4.99

THE FOUNDATIONS OF CHRISTIAN ENGLAND

THE FOUNDATIONS OF
CHRISTIAN ENGLAND

Augustine of Canterbury & His Impact

Anthony Marett-Crosby OSB

Ampleforth Abbey Press
(Distributed by Gracewing)

AMPLEFORTH ABBEY PRESS
AMPLEFORTH ABBEY
YORK
from
Gracewing
Fowler Wright Books
Southern Avenue, Leominster
Herefordshire HR6 0QF

Typeset at Ampleforth Abbey.
The text is set in 12pt Bembo (the headings in Perpetua).
Printed at the Cromwell Press, Broughton Gifford,
Melksham, Wiltshire SN12 8PH

ISBN 0 85244 434 6

CONTENTS

Introduction   1

Why a Mission?   5

Gregory   11

Augustine   16

The Journey   21

Augustine and Æthelberht   24

The Old and the New   26

Establishing a Church   33

Christians and Pagans   38

Augustine Again   42

Conclusion   45

Chronology   49

Further Reading   51

SHORT TITLES

Bede, *E.H.*	—	*Ecclesiastical History of the English People* St Bede the Venerable
Whitby	—	*Life of Pope St Gregory the Great* Anonymous
Constance, *V.G.*	—	*The Life of Germanus of Auxerre* Constance of Lyons
Gregory, *Reg.*	—	*Registrum Epistolarum* Gregory the Great
Gregory, *Dial.*	—	*The Dialogues* Gregory the Great
E.H.D.	—	*English Historical Documents vol. 1* ed. D. Whitelock (Eyre & Spottiswoode, 1955)

ACKNOWLEDGMENTS

The author would like to thank Br Colmán Ó Clabaigh for his help with this text. He would also like to thank Mrs Michelle Bennett, without whose assistance it would never have been completed.

THE FOUNDATIONS OF
CHRISTIAN ENGLAND

Introduction

THE year 1997 is a year of anniversaries. It is the fourteenth
centenary both of the arrival of the Roman missionary
Saint Augustine to Kent and of the death of the Irish exile Saint
Columba, the founder of the monastery at Iona. Augustine and
Columba are the twin hooks upon which the Christianity of
the this island hangs, for each in their own way contributed
hugely to the making of the Anglo-Saxon church. Each played a
part in producing that world of holiness, learning and mission
that for us is embodied in the historian and scholar Saint Bede.
Bede, Augustine, and Columba can moreover only be understood alongside a fourth figure, the Pope whose decision it was
to send Augustine and his companions to England. Saint
Gregory the Great was the guiding mind behind the mission,
and represented to Bede all that was finest in the tradition of the
Roman Church. Our story will therefore revolve around these
four saints, and if Augustine seems at its centre, in truth each
one is properly a centre in himself. This is not a straightforward
or unadorned history of Augustine, because we can only come
to Augustine through Bede and Bede relied in turn on Gregory
the Great for much of his information, just as Augustine had
relied on Gregory for advice and support. It is an attempt to see
Augustine in his context, the context in which one can understand him as the founder of Christianity in England.

That context inevitably predates the year 597 itself. The whole
Anglo-Saxon period is formed from an event that took place
around the year 410, when after nearly four centuries Roman
rule in Britain came to an end. Britain had been a significant and
strongly defended part of the great empire, a colony bordered

by the sea and, to the north, by Hadrian's Wall. For most purposes, Roman Britain stopped at that wall, and to the north lay the Picts who were with complete consistency the opponents both of the Romans and, in their turn, of the Anglo-Saxons. The Picts and the story of their conversion to Christianity lies outside our direct concern — they remained a presence and a threat on the northern border.

Inevitably, the effect of the Roman Empire upon Britain was huge. Amongst its many influences was Christianity, which came to England with the Romans and which bore fruit in the martyrdom of Saint Alban in the third-century. Though we know little of it, it is clear that there was an established Christian community in Britain at least by the year 314, when three British bishops attended a council in the Gaulish city of Arles. From the later actions of Saint Germanus, it is clear that the Christians of Britain continued to regard themselves as closely connected with the Church across the Channel.

The end of Roman Britain remains dark to historians. It seems that in the earliest years of the fifth-century the island was increasingly under attack from pagan barbarians whose homes lay in the lands of the northern European mainland. These invaders were known as the Saxons, and their reputation was fierce. After the Romans departed from their most northerly territory, the Saxon raids continued against the Britons, whose rulers at this time of conquest remain unknown to us. All we can say is that the Saxons, invading from the North Sea, settled in the east of what is now England, and the Britons retreated to the west. British kingdoms were established in the lands of Cornwall, Wales and the north-west, and the old unity of the Roman colony was sundered.

But the influence of Rome could hardly vanish after so long a period of occupation. Even under such a threat, enough of Christianity survived to warrant a visit from the Gaulish bishop Germanus in the year 429 to counter the threat of heresy. As the Saxons advanced, Christianity retreated with the British, but remained in those parts of the island to which the Saxons had never come. Thus there were still British bishops when Augustine came to England.

But if the British survived, it was the Saxons who were victorious. From the end of the fifth-century, there is evidence of the establishment of permanent Saxon kingdoms in England, kingdoms where the religious outlook was shaped by the traditions of Germanic paganism. It was to such a kingdom as this, where the ways of the Roman Empire had never held sway, that Augustine came in 597.

Before beginning the story of Augustine, a note on the sources for our account would not be inappropriate. Any historian of the period must rely in the first instance on the *Ecclesiastical History* of Saint Bede. Bede was born some seventy years after the arrival of Augustine, and completed his monumental *History* in 731. Though writing some time after the events and with particular concerns of his own, Bede is one of the great fathers of the writing of history, for he assiduously collected evidence for his *History* insofar as it was available to him. For the mission of Augustine, his principal source comes from Gregory the Great, from a selection of the letters of Gregory which he probably acquired from Canterbury. These letters form the second important source for the period, for Bede did not have access to the more complete collection of the Gregorian correspondence which is now available to historians. These two texts form the backbone of the study that follows, supplemented in certain areas by other written material and by archaeological finds. In many areas, this collection of evidence does not answer all the questions that we want to ask, but it represents nevertheless a uniquely well-documented episode in the history of what is commonly called the Dark Ages.

Why a Mission?

GREGORY'S decision to send Roman missionaries to England remains both momentous and a little opaque. Its consequences are clear enough, but if we ask why Gregory chose to send a mission to England at all, we find ourselves faced with a variety of answers. According to one tradition, Gregory's first encounter with the Anglo-Saxons was at a Roman slave-market, where he saw youths for sale, youths described by Bede as having 'fair complexions, handsome faces, and lovely hair'. Their appearance was so striking to Gregory that he was prompted to ask where they came from, and heard that they came from the island of Britain, where paganism still ruled. His reaction to this was to lament that men with such bright faces could live in such darkness as this, and when on further questioning he discovered that they were called Angles he responded that 'they have the appearance of angels, and such men should be fellow heirs of the angels in heaven'.*

It is a story with an excellent pedigree, for Bede took it from the same tradition as did the anonymous *Life of Pope Gregory* written by a monk of Whitby in the early decades of the eighth-century. Its author was not concerned directly with telling the story of the English mission, but he did see that mission as one of the main signs of Gregory's sanctity of life and ministry. He pictures Gregory going straight from the market to Pope Benedict to ask — indeed to beg — that he himself be sent as a missionary to England. The Pope agreed, and Gregory even set off on the long journey, but a combination of the anger of the people of Rome and miraculous signs forced him to turn back. It seemed that Rome could not do without him, so Gregory was forced to wait, dispatching missionaries himself as soon as he ascended the papal throne.

---

*   Bede, *E.H.* II.1 and Whitby 9-10

The linear progression from the meeting with the slaves to the sending of Augustine is elegantly clear in the Whitby *Life*. Bede, as has been said, also tells the story of the meeting with the Anglo-Saxon slaves, and he acknowledges it readily as part of the tradition he had received. He describes that meeting as 'the reason why he showed such earnest concern for the salvation of our race', clearly referring to the kind of chronology presented by the Whitby author. But Bede does not place the story of the meeting with the slaves chronologically before Augustine's mission. It is indeed only mentioned after the mission story has been told, almost as an aside within a chapter devoted to the various qualities of Gregory the Great. Whatever Bede thought of the story, however much he revered it as part of the tradition he had inherited, he did not use it as unequivocally as did his predecessor.

Yet we should not put the story aside merely out of a fashionable distrust of the picturesque. Bede does not make as much of it as did the Whitby *Life*, but a chance reference among the letters of Gregory the Great suggests that it may not be a mere fancy. One of Gregory's most frequent correspondents was the priest Candidus, who acted as the administrator of papal lands in Southern Gaul. In one of these letters, dated September 595, Gregory writes to his delegate to discuss the proper use of money raised by these estates.* There he encourages Candidus to use the money to purchase English boys aged 17 or 18, with the intention that they be sent to monasteries and therein given to God. We know nothing of Candidus's success in this venture, and Bede certainly cannot be blamed for omitting it as he did not have access to anything more than a selection of the Gregorian letters. It nevertheless suggests that there was a link between

---

* Gregory, *Reg.* VI.10

Gregory and Anglo-Saxon youths coming to Rome, a link that puts the story of his encounter with the slaves into a context.

Gregory's knowledge of such Anglo-Saxon youths may be connected to another theme within his letters which suggests that he understood the reasons for the mission in different terms. On at least two occasions, Gregory refers to the desire of Englishmen to come to know the faith, a desire of which he had become aware through channels unknown. Moreover, Gregory notes that 'the priests who are in the area do not have care for them', and at least part of the purpose of the mission may have been simply to provide such priests.* If Gregory could not rely on native British clergy, he could rely upon Augustine, and he certainly intended Augustine to recruit Frankish clergy to the cause during his journey through Gaul. Again, Bede did not know of these letters, but they add an element to our understanding of the reasons for the mission, stemming very much from Gregory himself.

For Bede himself, the reason for Augustine's mission to England is revealed by the context in which he places the story within his *Ecclesiastical History*. The fifteen chapters dealing with Augustine form a self-enclosed unit within his work, but they were nevertheless intended to be read in the context of what came before. What immediately precedes the Augustine story is the account of another missionary, the Gaulish Bishop Germanus.

Germanus, who lived from about 375 to 448, was not a missionary in the same sense as Augustine. He came from Gaul at the request of the native British clergy to a country that was regarded, by him and his biographer at least, as still Christian. His aim

---

* Gregory, *Reg.* VI.51 and VI.60

7

was not to spread the faith but to correct an error that had entered into it, an error that was to spread through many parts of the Western church under the label of Pelagianism. The doctrine of Pelagianism taught that man was able to work for his own salvation by his own efforts and apart from grace, and for much of the fifth-century it was judged to be the principal threat to true Christianity. Bede, following Germanus's biographer Constance of Lyons, tells us that this teaching had wide appeal amongst the British Christians, in part perhaps because Pelagius himself was British. So pervasive was its effect in the British Church of the mid fifth-century that help was summoned from overseas, and in 429 and again around the year 447 Germanus answered the appeal, crossing the Channel to preach against the heretics.*

Germanus is presented by Bede and by Constance as successful in this aim, though the fact he had to come over a second time may cast a shadow over the long-term effect of his first visit. He is portrayed as a powerful preacher, as a worker of miracles and as one able to bring military victory against the Scots. This last he achieved by teaching the British a new war cry, the triple *hallelujah*, which they used to great success. We may be sure that this public demonstration of power ensured theological as much as military victory. But for our purposes what is significant is not Germanus himself as much as the way in which Bede uses him as the preface to the mission of Augustine. It is in the context of both the similarities and the differences between the two missions that Bede wishes us to read the story of Augustine.

To some extent, Germanus and Augustine were doing the same work. The introduction to the 1844 English translation of the

---

* Bede, *E.H.* I.17-21, based on Constance, *V.G.* III.12-18 and V.25-27

Life of Germanus declares that 'next to the service of establishing primarily the Christian faith in a nation, none may deserve higher praise [than he]'. Its author, and probably Bede as well, felt that Augustine and Germanus were engaged alike in the service of the gospel, and each is presented by Bede as opposing a false way of thinking that, because of its falsity, lacked power. When Germanus confronted the Pelagian bishops, he demonstrated to them the superiority of his wisdom in preaching the gospel, and such was his obvious authority that the Pelagian bishops joined the people in begging Germanus to effect the cure of a blind boy. At least in part, this power rested on his status as an outsider, and here again there is a similarity with Augustine.

But in more significant ways Germanus and Augustine are very different. Though Germanus comes in from outside, he comes to a Christian country, whereas Augustine arrives in a predominantly pagan kingdom. Moreover, they represent two different kinds of holiness, and it may have been in Bede's mind to emphasise that one was, in the end, less successful than the other. Bede gets his account of Germanus from Constance, and selects from Constance those parts of Germanus's life relevant to the history of England. In consequence, the picture we are offered of Germanus is a partial one, and we hear nothing of his ascetic lifestyle or of his monastic foundation. These were in no sense important in his mission to England, where Germanus's witness to the faith is achieved by preaching and miracles but not by the way of life that he led. It is that way of life which in the mission of Augustine proves the greatest witness of all.

Germanus is successful, but only in a limited way. He leaves ecclesiastical peace but not civil peace, and the single chapter with which Bede links Germanus to Augustine is one in which strife and the abandonment of truth and justice dominate. Bede also tells us of the failure of the native British clergy to preach the faith to the new peoples, to the Angles and Saxons and other Germanic tribes who were crossing the sea in search of new lands. What is needed is not a new Germanus, but a new kind of missionary, who will not only bring the faith but will bring reconciliation as well.

Gregory

IF GERMANUS provides the context for Augustine, Gregory provides Bede with the reason. The whole of Bede's account of the Augustinian mission is dominated by the figure of the great Pope, whose presence is much more clearly felt than is that of Augustine himself. In part, this reflects Bede's use of Gregory's letters, of which he had a selection probably drawn from sources at Canterbury. Equally, Gregory embodied for Bede exactly the kind of bishop of which he approved, a man who was at once both monk and pastor. It is that combination of virtues that is for Bede the distinctive reason for the success of the Augustinian mission, and it is a combination derived from its initiator.

That any tradition survives about the early life of Gregory is due largely to the affection in which he was held by the English. Strangely for a Pope now regarded as so important in the wider history of the church, his first biographer lived not in Rome but in Whitby, and the earliest Roman *Life* was not composed until the pontificate of Pope John VIII at the end of the ninth-century. It is therefore from Whitby and other scattered references that some picture of his early life may be recovered.

Gregory was born around the year 540, in an Italy ravaged by Lombard invasions and imperial counter-invasions. Around the year 574 it seems that Gregory became a monk, rising soon to be one of the deacons of Rome and then becoming a papal ambassador to the court of the Emperor in Constantinople. He probably spent seven or eight years in this great city before being recalled to Rome, where it is traditionally thought he became abbot of the monastery of his profession. Gregory himself nowhere tells us that he did so, and the story comes from the late Roman *Life* composed by John the Deacon, but even if he did not take up that particular title, we may assume he had an authoritative position in a community which he himself had founded upon his own family estates. When John describes Gregory as an abbot, he is probably referring to Gregory's role as a father within that community, of which many stories are preserved. Later in his life, Gregory looked back to his years as a monk in the mon-astery of Saint Andrew as his happiest time. Writing in the preface to his *Dialogues*, he says:

> I remember with sorrow what I once was in the monastery, how I rose in contemplation above all changeable and decaying things, and thought of nothing but the things of heaven. ... But now, by reason of my pastoral care, I have to bear with secular business, and, after so fair a vision of rest, am fouled with worldly dust.*

Indeed, that vision of rest lasted for only four years after his return from Constantinople. In the year 590, at the death of Pelagius II, Gregory was elected to the Roman See, a position he held until his own death in the year 604.

Perhaps because of Bede, or because of the English love for their own history, Gregory has become known as the apostle of England, and of England alone. But this is to ignore a background to the mission of Augustine, a background that shaped its direction in important respects. For Gregory was not a one-time missionary. It was both natural to him and natural to his conception of the purpose of the Roman See that missionary work should have a high priority, and England was one among several endeavours in this work of conversion, albeit its most famous.

Some understanding of Gregory's attitude to mission may be seen in his approach to Judaism. Gregory recognised both the essential differences between Jews and Christians, and the fact

---

* Gregory, *Dial.* preface

that the position of Jews was protected under Roman Law. It is in the context of this second point that Gregory wrote 'we will not have the Hebrews oppressed and afflicted unreasonably'.*
Equally, the fact that they were not Christian made them appropriate objects of his zeal for souls. In the case of the Jews especially, Gregory's zeal translated itself not into force but into persuasion, and on those occasions when he heard that the Jews had been forcibly converted, he criticised those who so acted.
Writing to the Bishop of Arles he denounced the practice of forced conversion, and suggested an approach later to be exemplified in the mission to England. He wrote:

> I appeal to your fraternity to preach frequently to
> these persons and appeal to them in such a way that
> the kindness of the teacher more than anything else
> may make them desire to change their former mode
> of life.†

With this in mind, it is appropriate to turn to the most immediate background to the mission to England, Gregory's endeavours in the island of Sardinia. Three years before Augustine arrived in England, Gregory sent two commissioners to the island to execute a new initiative on his behalf. They were both to examine the work of the bishops there and to address the problem of paganism, working alongside the existing hierarchy but galvanising them into new action where before there appears to have been only passivity. Thus writing to Archbishop Januanus of Caralis, Gregory laid out his vision of the work of the missionary, emphasising vigilance, preaching, appropriate coercion and the use of the existing structures of the old imperial Christianity to

---

* Gregory, *Reg.* XI.6

† Gregory, *Reg.* I.45

effect the goal of conversion. Vigilance was to be exercised in identifying idol worshippers, soothsayers and magicians, and the bishop was to preach against these practices and those who performed them both by the presentation of doctrine and by the threat of eternal punishment. Coercion was also judged appropriate for those who refused to listen to such preaching, though it was to be measured coercion and shaped according to the particular state of life of the recalcitrant concerned. Thus slaves were to be chastised while freemen were to be held in prison. Gregory was in no doubt that there was an appropriate place for such measures, writing in justification of this:

> They who scorn to listen to the words of salvation which reclaimed them from the peril of death may at any rate by bodily torments be brought back to the desired sanity of mind.*

Moreover, the Church of Sardinia could use some of its long-established assets in pursuit of this goal. Gregory urged the bishops to ensure that no pagans lived on their episcopal estates, and he suggested that financial penalties might be applied to pagan tenants of church lands. It was to prove a potent combination of methods, for judging from Gregory's own correspondence they had by the year 600 achieved some measure of success. Gregory himself was especially elated at the conversion of the tribe of the Barbaricini, who he had once described as 'senseless animals who know not the true God but worship trees and stones'. Admittedly, their conversion was undoubtedly assisted by it being a term of a peace treaty they were forced to sign after a heavy military defeat, but Gregory nevertheless rejoices at this saving of souls, a goal so close to his heart.†

---

* Gregory, *Reg.* IX.204

† Gregory, *Reg.* IV.25 and *passim* IV.25-29

In comparing the Sardinian mission with that to England, we should note both similarities and differences. That there were similarities is clear, for in any mission directed to paganism similar problems would emerge, and similar solutions could be suggested. What is most striking is that in both cases Gregory made use of monastic missionaries, for Augustine had a monastic forerunner in the person of Abbot Cyriacus, one of the two original commissioners sent to Sardinia. Equally, in Sardinia as in England, Gregory made use of the secular arm, knowing that the work of princes was at least as important as the work of bishops.

But these similarities should not serve to conceal the real differences. Above all, Sardinia existed within that part of the Roman world in which the old institutions of imperial Christianity were alive, even if they needed a new injection of enthusiasm. In Sardinia, the Pope knew that there were bishops, even if they were inefficient, and that there were church lands even if they were inhabited by unconverted peasants. This represented a recognisable framework in which Gregory could operate, a framework which had once extended to Roman Britain but which had faded away long before the arrival of Augustine. Britain, with its new English settlers, was on the edge of the Roman thought world, and outside that part of the old Roman Empire where the structures of that once great state survived intact. England was far away, and the many letters that Gregory sent out to those whom Augustine met on his journey reveals how much the Pope had to rely upon the goodwill and support of others. It is inconceivable that the Gregorian mission to England would have worked without the support of the monarchy of Northern France, the Merovingians. If Sardinia was Gregory's backyard, Southern England was seen by the Merovingians as almost their own.

IF THE shadow of Gregory looms large over the English mission, Augustine is its principal actor. Yet for a figure of such significance, we know remarkably little of his background or character. What we have is gleaned from chance references in Gregory's letters and from Bede's account, and both texts tell the same story. What is essential to Augustine is that he and his companions were 'God-fearing monks'. It is Augustine's monastic identity that shapes the particular story of the English mission, and which makes him an altogether different kind of missionary to a figure like Germanus. Two of Gregory's letters give more details about this monastic background.* In the first place, Gregory tell us that he was 'brought up by a rule in a monastery', and we also hear that he was once 'the *præpositus* of my monastery'. *Præpositus* is the word used by Saint Benedict and other western monastic fathers to mean Prior, and we may therefore attach to Augustine something of the role of that official as envisaged in Benedict's *Rule*. Moreover, Augustine had acted as Prior in Gregory's own monastery, and we may therefore assume that his character both as monk and superior was well-known to the Pope.

What was this monasticism in which Augustine was trained? It is consonant with the lack of information we have about Augustine himself that we cannot answer this question directly. But whatever his monasticism was, it was that of Gregory, and in seeking to understand Augustine's monastic identity it is to Gregory that we must turn again. Gregory himself, of course, did not create Roman monasticism out of nothing. The early history of ascetic and monastic endeavours in and around Rome is dark, but a significant patch of light is that provided by the letters of Saint Jerome, who himself spent some years as a hermit in the Syrian

---

* Gregory, *Reg.* XI.37 and IX.223

desert before coming to the city. Jerome lived in Rome for nearly twenty years at the end of the fourth-century, and during that time he preached the ideal of the ascetic life with considerable effect. It was a message that he applied especially to women, whom he set up as urban ascetics in a manner that provoked both admiration and discomfort. For a while, Jerome dominated Christian Rome, and there is even some evidence that he expected to be elected to the Roman See, but it was not to be. Jerome's love for Rome grew as sour as Rome's love for Jerome had grown to anger, and in the early years of the fifth-century he left for Bethlehem, leaving behind him an ascetic tradition over which he continued to watch from his own monastery in the Holy Land.

Between Jerome and the years of Gregory we know little about the history of Roman monasticism. It is however clear that there were monastic rules, and Gregory's own *Dialogues*, written around the year 594, reveal a religious landscape in which monks and hermits flourished. Amongst these was Benedict, whose *Rule* was to come to be the single most formative document of Western monasticism. It is through Gregory that we know anything at all about the life of Benedict, and it is in the light of Gregory's description of Benedict that the link between the two men has been presumed. Certainly, Gregory does not conceal his admiration for Benedict, and the *Dialogues* do reveal that Gregory knew the *Rule*. He writes that:

> The man of God, amongst so many miracles for which he was so famous ... was also learned in divinity: for he wrote a *Rule* for his monks, both excellent for discretion and also eloquent for style. ... If any be curious to know further, he may in the institution of that *Rule* understand all his manner of

life and discipline, for the holy man could not otherwise teach than he himself lived'.*

Is it possible to draw from this paragraph the conclusion that
Gregory himself, and therefore Augustine, followed the *Rule of
Saint Benedict*? Modern scholars are divided on this question,
though one such has recently written that 'it is difficult to believe
that elements of Benedict's *Rule* were not in use at Saint
Andrew's'.† Others are rightly more cautious, but it seems fair to
conclude that all we know of Gregory's monasticism suggests
that he was formed in the same tradition that produced the *Rule
of Benedict*, even if he himself did not use it.

Gregory himself was not a monastic legislator. Within the body
of his letters, only two specific legislative provisions survive, reg-
ulating firstly the minimum age for an abbess and secondly that
the noviciate for monks should last two years.‡ But his letters
are peppered with references that demonstrate his zeal for the
monastic life, and his desire for it both to be extended by new
foundations and reformed. Gregory himself turned his Roman
family home into the monastery of Saint Andrew, and established
six other communities on his Sicilian estates. He constantly
encouraged others to found monasteries, and was equally zealous
in encouraging those in authority to reform communities where
observance had become slack. Gregory expected the bishops to
be as enthusiastic as himself in this work, and when he heard of
religious who had abandoned their monastic estate, he was not
slow to blame the bishops. Thus writing to the Bishop of
Sipontum he declares:

---

* Gregory, *Dial.* II.36

† J. Richards, *Consul of God* p.34 (see further reading)

‡ Gregory, *Reg.* IV.11 and X.9

Had you known how to comport yourself as guardian of the monastic life, or how to act as a bishop, the daughter of Tullianus ... would never have been allowed to throw off her monastic habit and resume secular dress. ... But inasmuch as you are sunk in excessive sloth and stupor, the crime has hitherto been left unpunished, to your great disgrace.*

This extract shows Gregory at his most uncompromising, but the stability of monks and nuns was not the only issue so to arouse his ire. Even before he was elected Pope, his attitude to monastic poverty was apparently harsh, and Gregory himself records a story in his *Dialogues* of a monk near death who told one of his brethren that there were three gold coins in his possession. When Gregory found this out, he abandoned his dying brother and ordered that he should not be buried with his community but thrown on a dung-hill with the three coins.† It is not a story that shows Gregory in an especially attractive light, but it belongs to a long tradition of such opposition to the keeping of private wealth by monks, and it is strongly reminiscent of Saint Benedict's own provisions against the vice of private ownership in the *Rule*.

But such attitudes only make sense in a wider context, the context of prayer and holiness. Here, Gregory cannot be faulted, for in his letters and especially in the *Dialogues* we encounter someone who sought holiness for himself and admired it in others. The whole purpose of the *Dialogues* was to demonstrate that holiness had not vanished from the Italy of the sixth-century, that

---

* Gregory, *Reg.* VIII.8

† Gregory, *Dial.* IV.55

prayer and ascetic endeavour could still bring a Christian to God. Thus when Bede describes Augustine as 'one who feared God' he was placing him in a tradition of Christian holiness which Gregory would have recognised immediately. Bede thereby ascribed to Augustine a monastic virtue much praised by Saint Benedict, who uses the phrase fifteen times in the course of the *Rule* in so wide a variety of contexts that it acts as a constant refrain in his understanding of monastic spirituality. If it does not give us the kind of detail about Augustine as a monk that we would like, it places him within a recognisable context of holiness, a context whose parameters were in large measure laid down for the Western church by Gregory.

The Journey

ONCE Gregory had decided to send his missionaries to England, they had to get there. Bede does not concern himself with the mechanics of this process, but Gregory was very much concerned to ensure that Augustine and his companions had the easiest possible journey, and gained appropriate help and support *en route*. Fourteen of the twenty-seven letters relating to England in Gregory's *Registrum* take the form of commendatory epistles relating to the various journeys undertaken by the missionaries to and from England in the first few years, and they reveal something of both the route they took and the problems they faced. It appears that they travelled first to the great monastery of Lérins, and from there moved on to Marseilles, Aix, Arles, Vienne, Lyons, Autun and on to the north. The final phase of their journey is not revealed by Gregory, though Bede tells us that they crossed the Channel and landed on the Isle of Thanet.*

The journey was not without its significant events. In the first place, it is clear that Augustine and his companions lost heart at one point and determined to abandon their venture. Gregory wrote to encourage them, telling them to pay no attention to 'evil-speaking tongues'.† It appears that Augustine returned to Rome in order to make their case, and he returned to his companions not simply as *præpositus* but now as abbot. It was a mark of confidence, and also of authority.

That authority was decisively advanced by Augustine's episcopal ordination. By reading Gregory alone, the evidence would point to his being consecrated during the journey, by the hands of bishops who could, however vaguely, be described as living in

---

* Bede, *E.H.* I.25

† Gregory, *Reg.* VI.53

German lands.* This raises two questions; firstly, why was Augustine ordained on his journey and not in Rome, and secondly, why does Bede tell such a different story? Bede describes Augustine receiving his ordination after the initial work of conversion was over, and records that he travelled to the city of Arles to receive the consecration. The descriptions given by Gregory and Bede cannot comfortably be harmonised, and historians have tended to prefer the chronology given by Gregory while retaining some uncertainty as to why it took place when it did. It seems reasonable, if not certain, to conclude that by the time Augustine came to England he was a bishop, ordained perhaps by some of those bishops whose help Gregory had sought through his letters.

It would be fascinating to know more from Gregory or Bede about the companions who travelled with Augustine, and whose fears were laid to rest by Augustine's nomination as an abbot. Later tradition has always identified them all as monks, and their tombs were venerated at Canterbury throughout the Middle Ages. In fact, Gregory himself does not say absolutely that they were all monks, and some of the forty who landed at Thanet were Frankish interpreters. Bede does reflect on the terror of the Romans amongst them at the prospect of going to England, a terror which reminds us that the new kingdom of Æthelberht was on the very edge of the consciousness of Rome. It was, very literally, the end of the world, and in despatching missionaries so far away, Gregory could not but elicit the support of a monarchy who at times regarded England as its own.

This monarchy was that of the Merovingians. Bede has little to say about the Merovingian involvement in Augustine's mission,

---

* Gregory, *Reg.* VIII.29 and Bede, *E.H.* I.27

but Gregory's letters demonstrate its importance both in Augustine's initial journey and thereafter.* It seems that the help of Queen Brunhild was especially important, for from 596 to 600 she was Regent of the kingdom, and had control over a foreign policy stretching from England to Constantinople. The affairs of the kingdom of Æthelberht would have seemed very close to home, the more so as Æthelberht had himself married a member of the Merovingian royal family. As Augustine passed through the court of Brunhild, he established contacts which were to prove of great importance when he came to meet the overlord of southern England.

---

* Gregory, *Reg.* VI.51, VI.60, VIII.4, IX.214, and XI.47-51

Augustine and Æthelberht

WHETHER Augustine was a bishop or not, we may be sure that when he landed in England he came face to face with a man possessed of a very different but no less real authority. Whether by fortune or planning, the Roman missionaries found themselves within the kingdom of the strongest Anglo-Saxon ruler of his day, whom Bede introduces as *rex potentissimus*, the most powerful king. According to Bede, the kingdom of Æthelberht extended from the Channel to the Humber; so when Augustine went to see him he faced not simply *a* king but *the* king.

It was for two reasons an advantageous encounter. Firstly, Æthelberht was, for all of his reign, in close contact with the Frankish Merovingian monarchy whose role has already been mentioned. Whether or not news of the mission had moved from one court to another, the path of Augustine to the presence of Æthelberht would undoubtedly have been smoothed by this Frankish contact. Augustine, moreover, brought with him both Frankish priests and Frankish interpreters, who spoke a language and followed ecclesiastical customs with which the kingdom of Kent was familiar. Secondly, Christianity was not unknown in the court of Æthelberht, for his Frankish bride Bertha was a practising Christian amidst the pagan court. Bede tells us that Bertha continued to practice her Christian faith with the assistance of a chaplain, the Frankish Bishop Liudhard. We know from Gregory's own letter to Bertha in the June of 601 that this Christian presence in the court of Kent was not unknown in Rome, and Bede gives us enough hints to allow us to imagine Bertha and her chaplain playing a role in that vital initial contact between missionary and monarch.[*]

---

[*] Bede, *E.H.* I.25 for all that follows

Bede does not record the details of that first encounter. At least, he does not record what Augustine had to say, save by way of a summary. All he tells us is that Augustine spoke of heaven on the one hand and Rome on the other. The good news was attached specifically to the promise of eternal rewards, and the source of that good news was never concealed. Furthermore, that first encounter was preceded according to Bede by prayer, a reminder once again of the monastic flavour that belongs to Bede's account of Augustine. But whatever was said and done, Æthelberht's response was uncertain. He declared that 'I cannot consent to accept ... and forsake those beliefs which I and a whole English race had held so long'. It was not exactly a rejection, but nor was it an immediate victory for the Romans. Æthelberht sent them to Canterbury, the seat of his government, there to live while he meditated upon what had been brought to him. It was to be there, at Canterbury, that the true conversion of England was to take place.

The Old and the New

IT IS here appropriate to consider briefly what it was that Æthelberht and his court were being asked to reject in favour of Christianity. However, any examination of the nature of Anglo-Saxon paganism at the dawn of Augustine's mission faces huge problems of evidence, for just as Bede is eloquent in describing the success of Christianity, by the same token he is highly reticent about giving any details of the paganism it challenged. For Bede, paganism was of no interest, and it is quite probable that he himself knew only the vaguest details about its cults or practices. The only purpose that the pagan religion serves in the *Ecclesiastical History* is as a straw man, set up in order to be demolished by the advent of Christianity. It is only with scattered and coincidental references that some picture of this paganism can be drawn, and then only in bare outline.

The clearest fact to emerge about this paganism from the pages of Bede is the existence of temples and shrines. Gregory the Great and Bede both speak of such temples, and Gregory's suggestion that they should be converted into Christian churches, a suggestion to be discussed later, indicates that they were not insubstantial structures. The best description we have of the workings of such a temple comes not from Æthelberht's southern kingdom but from the north, and is inserted by Bede as part of the narrative of the conversion of King Edwin of Northumbria by the missionary Paulinus.* Immediately following the conversion of Edwin himself, the King holds a council in which the high priest of the pagan religion, named Coifi, accepts Christianity and sets off to desecrate his once-honoured temple. Coifi had agreed to be the first to profane the old faith, and in a series of tantalising remarks Bede describes how he set about this. We are told first that Coifi took up arms and mounted a stallion, both of which

---

* Bede, *E.H.* II.13

had previously been acts forbidden to a pagan high priest. Having ridden to the shrine, Coifi proceeds to desecrate it by the simple expedient of casting a spear into it, a ritual act the significance of which it is hard to determine but which clearly had the effect of symbolising Coifi's abandonment of the old ways. Bede does not explain, perhaps because he did not know, why these actions undertaken by a pagan high priest would have had such ritual significance, but they give at least some glimpse of the world of pagan religion otherwise so opaque.

Some other details can be added to this picture. The first is the presence of idols, probably within the temple and probably made of wood or stone. Bede's language when speaking of pagan idols is, however, difficult to disentangle from Old Testament texts that preach against such idols, texts which Bede knew well and which colour his descriptions. There is also enough evidence to say that sacrifices took place in or near these temples, most probably sacrifices of animals. These may also have been connected to the practice of divination, known to have taken place and known to have been amongst the most enduring features of the pagan religion.*

If Bede is firm in his purpose that paganism should remain two-dimensional in his *History*, it is because he wants to emphasise the chasm that existed between Christianity and paganism, the exact image of that chasm between truth and falsehood. But there are some indications that the chasm may not have appeared quite so great to some in the decades immediately after the Augustinian mission. Above all, there is the evidence arising from the aposta-sy of King Rædwald of Kent. Rædwald is first mentioned by Bede as the successor of Æthelberht to the overlordship of south-

---

*   Bede, *E.H.* III.30 and III.22 for idols, II.15 for sacrifices

ern England, and he very probably exercised this dominion between the end of the fifth-century and the year 616.* More than any other of these overlords, the authority of Rædwald's kingship is apparent to us, especially if we accept the suggestion that the Sutton Hoo ship is his cenotaph. This great ship-grave, discovered in 1939 near Woodbridge in Suffolk, presents the most powerful archæological impression of Anglo-Saxon kingship that we have. And while it is true that no conclusive evidence allows us to identify it with Rædwald himself, the presence of Christian symbols among so evidently a pagan grave has suggested to many scholars a parallel with Bede's own account. For Bede's concern is not with Rædwald's power but with his syncretism, his maintenance of both Christianity and paganism at one and the same time. Bede writes that:

> After the manner of the ancient Samaritans, he seemed to be serving both Christ and the gods whom he had previously served. In the same temple he had one altar for the Christian sacrifice and another small altar on which to offer victims to devils. Ealdwulf, who was ruler of the kingdom up to our time, used to declare that the temple lasted until his time and that he saw it when he was a boy.

Bede's own attitude to this attempt to maintain both faiths hardly needs amplifying. His account does, however, preserve the only clear example of such syncretism within the decades following Augustine's mission, and it suggests that to Rædwald at least, Christianity and paganism were not irreconcilably opposed.

---

* Bede, *E.H.* II.15 for what follows

If the chasm, however large or small it appeared, was to be crossed, it is clear that Christianity needed to demonstrate the superiority of its power. Here, the confrontation between paganism and Christianity was not so different to that between orthodoxy and heresy already seen in the example of Germanus. He had proved the greater validity of orthodoxy in the sight of God by working a miracle in the presence of the Pelagian bishops, and Augustine was to do the same when confronted in his turn by the bishops of native British Christianity. But more important than any rivalry within Christianity was this confrontation with the powers outside it, powers that Bede ascribes time and again to the devil. In short, Christianity needed to demonstrate that it was of more worth than the religion it sought to replace, and almost all of the conversion accounts preserved by Bede contain some element of this. It is put at its clearest by Coifi, speaking in the council of King Edwin:

> If the [pagan] gods had any power they would have helped me more readily, seeing that I have always served them with greater zeal. So it follows that if, on examination, these new doctrines which have now been explained to us are found to be better and more effectual, let us accept them at once without delay.*

Coifi here points to two elements: the doctrines themselves are to be examined and adjudged as better or worse than those of paganism, but equally they are to be tested at the bar of efficacy, at the bar of power. It is a process we see at work in the case of Augustine and in many later conversions described by Bede. Thus it is seen in reverse in the year 664, when amongst other

---

* Bede, *E.H.* II.13

29

great events the plague hit the East Saxon kingdom of King Sighere. His reaction to the onset of plague was to desert Christianity, to restore the derelict temples and to worship the images contained in them, surely because these old symbols were judged a better protection in time of disaster. The East Saxons were reconverted by the preaching of Bishop Jaruman, and it has been suggested that the success of his preaching may well reflect the end of the plague.[*]

Clearest of all is the example of the preaching of Bishop Wilfrid to the West Saxons in the years after 678, for the West Saxons had not simply apostatised but had never been converted, were 'still in the bonds of heathen practices' according to Bede. Wilfrid's preaching is described as converting them to the faith, but also rescuing them from a three-year drought. It was an outward symbol of the efficacy of the baptismal waters that Bede could not ignore, for 'on the very day on which the people received the baptism of faith, a gentle but ample rain fell'. Not only did Wilfrid's preaching bring them relief from drought, but Bede also describes how he taught them to fish. The West Saxons apparently knew only how to fish for eels, but Wilfrid showed them how to use their nets to catch more appealing food, himself catching three-hundred such fish in the first attempt. It is a homely story but with a parallel in the Gospel accounts of Jesus's catches of fish that reminds us of its role as a demonstration of power and of the superior power of Christianity.[†]

Yet the power exercised by Augustine was to be both like and unlike that of Wilfrid. He was a worker of miracles, but he was

---

[*] Bede, *E.H.* III.30

[†] Bede, *E.H.* IV.13

also to convert by another more powerful means. It is appropriate therefore to return to our narrative, to return to Canterbury.

In some senses, the chapter in which Bede records the conversion of Æthelberht and others of the kingdom of Kent is an anticlimax.* There is no great oration from Augustine, no knock-down arguments which force the truths of Christianity upon those who heard. It is not a second Pentecost. This sense of anticlimax is so clear that it must be deliberate, and it is so portrayed in order to establish an essential element in Bede's understanding of the story. What converted Æthelberht was a combination of both preaching and the apostolic way of life, what Bede describes as 'the pure life of the saints'. It was the witness of the lives of the missionaries as much as what they say that mattered, and Bede thus described the converts as 'marvelling at their simple and innocent way of life and the sweetness of their heavenly promises'. These two elements, especially when conjoined to a third, the presence of miracles, define the true apostle for Bede. The truth of what Augustine was saying was confirmed both by how he lived and by the empowered actions that he undertook. The impact of these three elements — life, word and sign — proved enough to sway the king.

We gain some sense of the scale of this achievement from a letter written by Gregory to the Patriarch of Alexandria in the summer of 598. Gregory there tells him how he had sent a monk of his own monastery to England, of the miracles that accompanied his mission and of the baptism on Christmas Day of ten thousand Angles whose souls had now been saved for Christ. He assures the Patriarch that the prayers of the people of Alexandria had influenced these far away events and urges him to rejoice.†

---

* Bede, *E.H.* I.26 for all that follows   † Gregory, *Reg.* VIII.29

While we may not necessarily accept the figure he gives as entirely dispassionate, there can be little doubt that something great had taken place.

Establishing a Church

SUCH conversions were only the very first step on the long road towards establishing some permanent structure for the faith that Augustine had brought from Rome. In part, this was a question of resources, and Bede tells us that Augustine did not wait long before requesting reinforcements from Gregory.* We are told that after the manner of the Gospels, Augustine advised the Pope that the harvest was great but the labourers few, and in response there came a second group of missionaries, amongst whom were Mellitus, Justus, Paulinus and Rufinianus. All of these play their own not inconsiderable roles in the on-going story of conversion after Augustine, and they must have represented a real assistance in the work of the Canterbury community.

But Gregory did not restrict his assistance to labourers alone, even labourers such as these. Bede records that 'he sent with them all such things as were generally necessary for the worship and ministry of the church', including all the necessary furnishings for the sacramental life, relics and manuscripts. The inclusion of relics in this list may appear odd, but there was nothing which more firmly established a sense of continuity between old and new churches for Dark Age Christians than the physical presence of saints venerated in the mother church. Rome was becoming in this period the great centre of relics, and Bede's own monastery was later to be richly endowed with such memorials of the apostles by its founder, Benedict Biscop. To Augustine, the relics and the other gifts provided not only for immediate material needs but established an evident link between Canterbury and Rome, a link that was critically to shape his confrontation with the bishops that remained of the native British church.

---

* Bede, *E.H.* I.29 for what follows

This decisive encounter with the bishops is one of the very few sections in Bede's account of the mission not dependent upon Gregory.* The story is straightforward; Augustine organised a meeting at a place called Augustine's Oak, where he encouraged them to join in the work of conversion upon which he was engaged. The only condition attached to this was that the British bishops should adopt the Roman method of calculating Easter, that same issue which was to divide Roman from Celt seventy years later at the Synod of Whitby. Bede describes this encounter as 'a long and wearisome struggle', which Augustine attempted to resolve by the kind of contest in spiritual power that had proved so effective for Germanus. Just as in the Germanus encounter with the native British bishops, a blind man is brought before them, and once again it is the outsider, in this case Augustine, who is able to effect the cure. Bede does not tell us that the British bishops ignored or refused to accept this sign, but it did not lead to an immediate change. Rather, the British bishops sought and received time to consult with those whom they represented, and a second meeting was arranged. This was to prove even more ill-fated than the first.

The story of the second encounter between Augustine and the British is perhaps the most curious in the entire account of the mission. It is so because it contains the only apparent criticism of Augustine that we have, and it is a criticism that strikes at the heart of Augustine's monastic identity. Before coming to the meeting, the British consulted a hermit, the kind of holy man of whose achievements the *Dialogues* of Gregory the Great abound. The hermit gives the bishops a simple test to apply to Augustine, to test whether he is of God or of men. It is the test of humility, based upon whether Augustine rises at the arrival of

---

* Bede, *E.H.* II.2

the bishops or remains seated, thereby not acknowledging their authority. From all that Bede has said about Augustine's way of life, it might have seemed an easy test to pass, but Bede tells us that Augustine did not rise, and that the bishops 'setting him down as a proud man, strove to contradict everything he did'. What is most curious of all is that Bede does not explain this action on Augustine's part, neither excusing nor justifying him. Augustine is presented not merely as failing the test of humility, but also as adding new demands to his original position. Augustine asked the bishops on the second occasion not only to keep Easter according to the Roman calendar but to perform baptism according to the Roman rite. They refused, telling Augustine that they would not accept him as archbishop and would continue to practise in the manner of their own tradition. Augustine's response was to prophesy imminent military defeat as a consequence of their decision, a defeat which Bede tells us was not long in coming.

Augustine's approach to this encounter must count as amongst the most difficult elements in the mission story. Bede's source for the narrative is unknown, but it seems likely that it was originally critical of Augustine, and that Bede retained at least part of this criticism by incorporating the story of the hermit's advice and Augustine's proud behaviour. The story is also, of course, critical of the British, who by a clear judgement of God are the eventual losers. Bede writes that Augustine's prophecy of disaster 'through the workings of divine judgement came to pass in every particular as he had foretold'. In short, no one emerges with much credit from the meetings at Augustine's Oak, and the issue of reconciliation between the Roman and the British churches was to be left unresolved, a problem with which Augustine's successors would have to wrestle.

With the exception of this long chapter on Augustine's encounter with the British, everything that Bede has to say about Augustine's work in establishing his fledgling church is taken from Gregory. Indeed, almost all that Bede has to say about Augustine's work after the conversion is extracted from six of Gregory's letters. This is a curious fact, perhaps indicating that Augustine's work was less well-known in England in Bede's own day than Bede would like us to believe. Nevertheless, Gregory's letters do provide a unique glimpse of Augustine and the problems he faced, and while we only have Gregory's side of the correspondence, the three issues that dominate Gregory's letters allow us to see both the problems he faced and the solutions he advanced.

The first of these letters is the most curious of them all. It has become known as the *Libellus Responsionum* or *Answer Book*, and contains the text of nine questions raised by Augustine and the answers given by Gregory.* Its history as a letter is uncertain, though most historians accept that it is what Bede says it is, namely an authentic Gregorian text. The nine questions can be summarised under three broad headings, each of which is then taken up in a separate letter given by Bede in the chapters that follow. The whole section appears to have been carefully constructed, and the three main issues raised are worth a brief examination.

The first of them covers the question of episcopal government. Two particular problems raised by Augustine were how bishops should live with their clergy, and whether a bishop could be consecrated without other bishops being present. They reflect paradigm concerns of a fledgling church, and while Gregory's

---

* Bede, *E.H.* I.27

36

answers contained in the *Libellus* were undoubtedly sufficient for immediate needs, the long term demanded the proper establishment of a hierarchy. This need was addressed by Gregory in a letter of June 601, when he established two provinces centred on London and York, each with their own 12 suffragan bishops.[*] Curiously, Gregory nowhere refers in this letter to Canterbury, and he clearly envisaged that Augustine would establish the archiepiscopal seat of southern England in London. Whatever else was established, this never took place, presumably because Augustine recognised the political realities of seventh-century Kent much more clearly than did Gregory. That Canterbury survived as the primatial see of England is the clearest example of the political acumen of Bede's saintly bishop.

But the establishment of a hierarchy could only proceed successfully if that new hierarchy had some clear relationship to the bishops of Gaul. The connections between Gaul and southern England in this period have already been noted, and two of the questions contained in the *Libellus* touch directly upon this issue. The first relates to the different manner of celebrating Mass in the Roman and Gallic Churches, to which Gregory replies that Augustine is to make a careful selection from the customs of both for England. The second question relates to the authority of Augustine over the Gaulish Church, and here Gregory is unequivocal — he has no such authority, though he is to amend any faults he finds by persuasion. Gaul and England are, in Gregory's mind, to pursue separate paths, always closely related but with their own proper establishment. It is an issue raised again in another Gregorian letter cited by Bede, which again gives Augustine no real authority over Gaul.[†]

---

[*]   Bede, *E.H.* I.29 with Gregory, *Reg.* XI.39

[†]   Gregory, *Reg.* XI.45 with Bede, *E.H.* I.28

Christians and Pagans

THE third of the over-arching issues raised in the correspondence presented by Bede looks in a different direction. If the first two issues are concerned broadly with the formation of a new church, the third relates to the relationship of that church with its pagan environment. In the *Libellus*, this revolves around questions of marriage, and most especially which degrees of marriage are to be accepted. Gregory's answer was unusually permissive, causing considerable difficulty to canonists of later generations, and it reflects a sense of accommodation which is to be found most famously in Gregory's letter to Abbot Mellitus.*
Mellitus was one of the second wave of missionaries sent from Rome to assist Augustine, and to him Gregory wrote a letter enshrining that nuanced approach to the question of conversion which had worked on other missions. Now it is applied to native English paganism, and he warns Mellitus that the shrines of the pagan gods ought not to be destroyed. Rather, after they have been blessed with water, they should be used for the celebration of Mass. Gregory sees this as a way of using familiar places in order to encourage the people to worship the only God, much as the people of Israel in the Old Testament were given familiar things that led them into a deeper relationship with the God of Moses.

This remarkable letter to Mellitus can only be understood, however, in the context of Gregory's letter to Æthelberht.† Here a very different message seems to be being presented, one much more in tune with Gregory's advice to Sardinia. Æthelberht is to conform himself to the model of the first and greatest Christian emperor, Constantine, whose Christianity led to him to transcend former princes in renown. Æthelberht is specifically

---

* Gregory, *Reg.* XI.56 with Bede, *E.H.* I.30

† Gregory, *Reg.* XI.37 with Bede, *E.H.* I.32

required to act to suppress pagan cults, including the destruction of shrines. Gregory understands this as part of his duty to extend the faith among his subjects, in pursuit of which he is to listen carefully to the advice of Augustine, through whom God will work.

The letters to Æthelberht and Mellitus reveal two sides of Gregory's vision of the Christian mission to paganism. On the one hand, his desire for accommodation was realistic, but equally he knew that the support of secular princes was vital for the Church to achieve her aims. The advice to Mellitus appears to conflict with that of Æthelberht because in a real sense the roles of the two elements in the mechanism of conversion were different. If the royal hand is pushed and the ecclesiastical hand restrained, the balance might be right. It is a distinction that Gregory wants to maintain.

This account of the Gregorian position on paganism in England should be placed alongside two pieces of information dating from the decades after Augustine. Firstly, we should note that the first royal edict we have that orders the destruction of pagan temples dates from the year 640, a generation after Gregory advised Æthelberht to eliminate the outward signs of paganism. Secondly, it is striking that those seventh-century law codes that have survived are strangely silent about paganism; there is no reference at all to the relationship between paganism and the state in the laws of Æthelberht, Hlothhere of Kent, or Ine of the West Saxons. Only in the laws of Wihtred of Kent do we see any sign of a king attempting to legislate against paganism in a law referring rather vaguely to 'sacrifices to devils'.* This post-Augustinian evidence suggests that it was Gregory's advice to

---

*   *E.H.D.* I p.363

Mellitus, rather than that to Æthelberht, that became the domi-
nant policy in the early decades of Christian southern England,
at least in terms of there being no obvious attempt to suppress
paganism from above.

What is less easy is to determine whether Gregory's suggestion
that the temples of the pagan cults be converted into Christian
churches was ever adopted. The evidence from the reign of
Rædwald has already been indicated, and no other textual evidence allows us to judge with certainty either way. Here,
archæological evidence may help, for scholars have identified at
least one site where a pagan structure does seem to have been
converted for Christian usage. The evidence comes not from
the kingdom of Æthelberht but from the kingdom of Edwin in
the north, where it was not Augustine but Paulinus who led the
work for conversion. A Northumbrian site at Yeavering does
show some sign of having been adapted in the manner envisaged by Gregory, and while not providing a firm foundation for
any conclusion, it does point in the direction of his letter to
Mellitus rather than that of the letter to Æthelberht.

In concluding this discussion of the relationship between
Christianity and paganism, three conclusions are available. The
first, that paganism was swept away quickly and radically, seems
not to fit the evidence available and nor does its reverse, that
Christianity simply merged into a predominantly pagan *milieu*.
A better conclusion lies in between, and it seems reasonable to
say that paganism and Christianity existed alongside each other
for some time, perhaps with some pagan sites being adopted for
Christian usage. Over time, the influence of paganism contract-
ed, though in popular superstition and divination its influence
seems to have endured. It is worth remembering that in the time
of Bishop Wilfrid, not far off a century after the arrival of

Augustine, there were still some parts of southern England where Christianity was unknown. Bede never highlights this, but any judgement of Augustine's own achievement must be shaped by the understanding that his work was the beginning of the process of conversion and not the end.

Augustine Again

WHAT part did Augustine himself play in this work of conversion? Bede does not go into details, and save for the meeting at Augustine's Oak he relies for his account almost entirely on the letters from Gregory, as has been seen. One of these letters, however, does offer a glimpse of Augustine at work, and it has rightly been judged a letter of significance not merely in the context of the mission but in the wider history of spirituality.* It begins by citing the first lines of the *Gloria*, and goes on to rejoice at the expulsion by Augustine's preaching of the darkness of pagan error. It praises all the aspects of that work of conversion that have been already indicated — preaching, prayer, and the replacement with Christian symbols of the idols of paganism. But it then goes on to focus on one very particular aspect of that work, the presence of miracles. Gregory writes to Augustine that:

> I know that the omnipotent God out of love for you
> has worked great miracles through you for the race
> which it was his will to have among the chosen.

The presence of miracles in the account of the mission should not surprise us. Indeed, they play a much smaller role with Augustine than in comparable accounts of other missionary saints, and in the whole story there survive only two miracles, both of which occur in the chapter on his encounter with the British bishops. Gregory's reaction to the news of Augustine's miracle working was a carefully nuanced welcome buttressed by a strong warning against the dangers of pride that lay before him. Gregory clearly feared that Augustine, secure in the knowledge of his own power, would lose that sense of dependence upon God which is the foundation of humility, and would instead sink

---

* Gregory, *Reg.* XI.36 with Bede, *E.H.* I.31

into humility's opposite, the sin of pride. Furthermore, Gregory clearly did not regard miracles as being a central tool in the armoury of conversion, and he knew that to base any mission upon such power alone was dangerous if only because miracles could be worked as much by those who were not Christians as by those who were. It is love that is for Gregory the true sign of the Christian, just as it is only because of the love of God that Augustine was granted the power to work his miracles at all.

But Gregory never regards the miracles as in themselves wrong. Their role in the work of Germanus is a reminder that the miraculous was an essential part of Dark Age religion, whether pagan or Christian, and to some degree Augustine had to be a miracle-worker if he was to succeed. This has already been seen as an important element in his initial meeting with the British bishops, and its significance for pagans is eloquently witnessed by Coifi.

Why then was Gregory so reluctant to allow Augustine's miracles to play a more prominent part in the mission? Gregory had, after all, exalted the presence of the miraculous in those saints he describes in his *Dialogues*, where miracles and prophecies are presented as the stuff of holiness. The point is that in the *Dialogues*, and in other passages where Gregory treats of miracles, the external signs of God's power are never an end in themselves. They always lead inwards, into the hearts of those who witness them and those who practice them. Thus what Gregory wanted to ensure with Augustine is that his soul was protected from that most un-monastic of vices: pride. Equally, he was concerned that the faith of those who witnessed these miracles should not rest upon this testimony alone, but on the altogether more durable witness of the preaching and the lives of the missionaries.

43

If our impression of Augustine is largely constructed from references in Gregory's letters, its final crafting is the achievement of Bede. For Bede, Augustine is presented first of all as a monk, establishing a monastery and achieving conversion by the life he lived. On the other hand, Bede accepts that Augustine is a man of power, who engages in and wins contests designed to prove spiritual authority. These two elements are not contradictory but together form Bede's model of what a monk-bishop should be. It is sometimes forgotten that Augustine is Bede's first such example, his first didactic tool in expressing his view of what bishops should be. In this sense, Augustine is the precursor of the fulness to come, the forerunner to that greatest of monk bishops, Bede's beloved Cuthbert.

Conclusions

THERE is an irony in this succession. Saint Cuthbert was not of Augustine's Roman stock, and had been formed in an altogether different tradition. In assessing the achievement of Augustine, we cannot neglect that other mission started by Columba, who abandoned his native Ireland and settled at Iona around the year 563, more than 30 years before Augustine arrived at Canterbury. Around the year 634, the new Christian King Oswald sent to Iona for help in furthering Christianity in his kingdom, and from Iona came Aidan, the founder of the community on Lindisfarne. It was Lindisfarne and the traditions of that community that became the crucible of English Christianity in north-east England.

In this great age of Anglo-Saxon Christianity, Augustine and the Rome from which he came were never forgotten, but Augustine himself was on the margin of its memory. It is significant that Bede tells the story of Augustine largely from a Roman perspective, through the letters of Gregory the Great. The missionary pope was never forgotten, as the Whitby *Life* demonstrates, but his envoy was less clearly remembered, perhaps because his own work of conversion was geographically limited. This is especially the case in comparison with those other missionaries inspired not by Gregory but by Columba, namely Aidan and Cuthbert. Alongside this tradition, Augustine's achievement seems real enough, but perhaps colourless and undramatic.

As long as we remain rooted to an English perspective this conclusion stands. But there is another conclusion from another perspective in which Augustine assumes a greater significance. If it is through Gregory that Bede comes to Augustine, then perhaps we too can come to a clearer understanding of Augustine's achievement not from England but from Gregory's own city of

45

Rome. It is indeed from the Roman perspective that Augustine's mission was most successful.

The background to understanding this Roman perspective on Augustine comes from the East. The first fifty years of the seventh-century saw some of Christianity's most ancient centres falling into the hands of Islam. By 650, the patriarchates of Jerusalem, Antioch and Alexandria had fallen into the hands of this new power, and Eastern Christendom had shrunk almost beyond recognition. Moreover, Rome itself had come under continued barbarian attack in the fifth- and sixth-centuries, and was hardly free from danger itself during the pontificate of Gregory. His relations with the Lombards, the new rulers of Italy, demonstrate what a careful hand the Roman See had to play in an Italy where the power of the Empire had decisively waned.

In this context, the fact that Rome turned in a new direction is of the utmost significance. Under Gregory, Rome shifted its gaze away from the Eastern Empire of Constantinople and towards the West and the North. The involvement of the papacy in Spain is one example of this, but the role of Gregory in England is the clearest example of all. The fact that the papacy was consulted over details of church organisation in a far-away land can be over-emphasised, but it does mark a new step in the history of Rome and the West. It gave the papacy a new focus, a focus that enabled it to respond in the eighth-century to new missionary work, much of which came from the Anglo-Saxons themselves. In 718, when the English missionary Saint Boniface came to Rome to gain approval for his mission to Germany, the papacy was used to looking North. That habit was largely the achievement of Augustine.

Moreover, England never forgot its link with the Christianity of Rome. Bede's account of the work of Archbishop Theodore and his successors demonstrates how far Canterbury looked to the South, but even in the North there was an attitude of mind that can be called 'Roman'. It is illustrated in evidence of pilgrimage, of relics, and of the adoption of the Roman dating of Easter at Whitby in 664. This outlook fused with that other tradition that came to the north from Ireland, and they were traditions that merged much more successfully than they ever clashed. It was the Irish who brought monasticism to the north of England, but it was Rome that inspired the early abbots of Wearmouth and Jarrow. In this sense, Augustine's greatest achievement was the world of Bede.

Chronology

*c.*410	The Romans leave Britain.
429	First journey of Germanus.
430	Death of Augustine of Hippo.
*c.*447	Second journey of Germanus.
*c.*456	The Britons desert Kent.
527	A major Germanic invasion, leading to the formation of some of the new kingdoms of England.
c. 540	Benedict writes his *Rule.*
563	Columba settles at Iona.
590	Election of Gregory I (the Great) to the See of Rome.
597	Augustine arrives in Kent. Death of Columba.
604	Death of Gregory.
*c.*604-5	Death of Augustine.
664	Synod of Whitby adopts the Roman dating of Easter
*c.*672-3	Birth of Bede.

Further Reading

PRIMARY SOURCES

Bede the Venerable, *The Ecclesiastical History of the English People* ed. B. Colgrave and R.A.B. Mynors (Oxford Medieval Texts, 1969). (Also in Penguin, tr. L. Shirley-Price, 1955.)

Gregory the Great, *Registrum Epistolarum* ed. D.L. Norberg (*Corpus Christianorum Series Latina* 140 and 140A, Brepolis 1982).

RECOMMENDED SECONDARY LITERATURE

N.P. Barry, *St Benedict & Christianity in England* (Ampleforth Abbey Press, 1995).

J. Campell (ed.), *The Anglo-Saxons* (Phaidon Press, Oxford 1982).

M. Deanesly, *Augustine of Canterbury* (Nelson, London 1964).

D.H. Farmer (ed.), *Benedict's Disciples* (Gracewing, 1995).

H.M.R.E. Mayr-Harting, *The Coming of Christianity to Anglo-Saxon England* (Batsford, 1972).

J. Richards, *Consul of God* (Routledge & Kegan Paul, 1980).